AF252133

Reflections of a White Bear

Winner of the 1993 Pearl Chapbook Contest
Judged by R. Nikolas Macioci

CAROLYN E. CAMPBELL

REFLECTIONS
OF
A WHITE BEAR

Pearl
Editions

1994

*To Velox, the white polar bear, in captivity
at the Denver Zoo from 1938 to 1959 . . .*

Pearl Editions
3030 E. Second Street
Long Beach, California 90803

Contents

As I read the entries for *Pearl's* 1993 chapbook contest, I kept asking myself if I was being unreasonable to expect more than writing can deliver from a single book of poetry. Then one Saturday night, I read for the first time Carolyn E. Campbell's *Reflections of a White Bear* and knew that my expectations had been met. I had found not only the winner but poetry that fulfills its promise as beautifully as writing will allow.

Campbell has achieved a breathtaking miracle of language in *Reflections of a White Bear*. Her book exudes that rare and mystifying feeling of an entity that has sprung into existence as a whole. Even in discussing this five-part poem it is difficult to know where best to enter the closed circle of perfection she has created. Appropriate imagery, exact details, harmonious sound, form suitable to content, and an unobtrusive yet strong narrative voice are elements Campbell melds together in much the same seamless way that a composer orchestrates the parts of a symphony.

From the opening line, "I sit on the balcony that hangs/ over the steamy Brazilian street,/ nursing Jason . . . " until the end of the book when a prayer for light is offered, the speaker reveals through unsentimental observations what it means to feel trapped, isolated, and lonely.

Not only are Jason and his mother "new together, vulnerable," but so are we new to her world and made consequently vulnerable as the mother leads us into her neighborhood. Pregnant One, Black Man, Red Coat, Screamer, The Gimp, Old Legs, and The Watcher are but a handful of residents in the human parade that Campbell's speaker observes from her balcony each day. For a day and a half, through the speaker's eyes, we see these people in exquisite detail:

> Pregnant One curls half way around her belly
> like a rubbery pod, split, guarding a single seed.

Yet these are not the only beings on whom she depends for a partial definition of her own existence. At the center of her life, in addition to Jason, are Robert and a white bear. Without angst, without resentment, and without enmity, the speaker interweaves information depicting the nature of her relationship with Robert, whom we assume to be Jason's father. On the first page we are told much in single stanza:

> Robert left this morning
> without waking me
> or saying goodbye.
> We never make love.
> We are polite.

Thereafter, the reader has occasion to gather additional clues that substantiate the emptiness of this relationship:

> Your wonderful eyes were shut
> and I was glad.
> When they are open,
> I search to see me reflected.
> I'm not there.
> Nothing is there.
>
> You are polite.
> I am polite.
> How terrible it is to be polite
> among friends,
> even worse among lovers.

At breakfast, "two ship-wrecked people" are "hoping for a rescue," and the explicit meaning of the statement "Good night, Robert . . . wherever you are" reverberates throughout the book.

It is, however, Velox, the blind, white bear, who is the unifying presence. Velox is not just a conspicuous symbol. He is real, and Campbell's expert description brings him to life:

> He'd stop and sway, swing
> his heavy pendulum head
> back and forth,
> then throw his nose high
> in the air hoping
> to catch a cold current . . .

From the speaker's viewpoint, the bear is real in yet another way: "Grandmother, I think the white bear is lonely." This loneliness is our own, because as we have been told by the speaker's grandmother:

> " . . . Velox is our teacher.
> He is our mirror, our reflection.
> What we see in the bear
> is what we see in ourselves."

The speaker is not like Velox because she can see, but she is like the white bear in that she exists in her own kind of captivity, pacing "five steps to the right . . . / five steps to the left . . . " as all of us do in our daily lives and in our philosophical reach for answers to "why's that clack together/ like dry sticks . . . "

An urgency rages within questions the woman on the balcony asks, but we never hear her scream for answers. Quietly she persists in observing, in putting together the pieces of life that surround her, so that, ultimately, this book is about hope. Underlying the discouraging observations is light. In fact, light imagery leads us through *Reflections of a White Bear* until we are guided at the end to a place where things " . . . All . . . at once, make sense." Campbell coalesces Robert, Jason, Grandmother, the cast of characters on the street, the white bear, and light itself into a brilliant conclusion that elevates the reader into a kind of personal fulfillment, a place where there really is an answer that stays in the reader's mind, not only while reading this marvelous, book-length poem, but ever afterwards.

—R. Nikolas Macioci
January, 1994

I. *Late Afternoon*

I sit on the balcony that hangs
over the steamy Brazilian street,
nursing Jason, feeling the rhythmic tug
on my breast, the velvet lips closing
around my nipple like a sea anemone
drawing it into its sea-salt mouth,
a primitive organ reacting
to the push-pull of milky tides,
the in and out pulse of sucking.
I am of this ocean,
host to this mouth,
a stem to this fleshy blossom.
We are new together, vulnerable,
and so I wrap the blanket around
this body to give it a shell.

In this heavy afternoon weighted by dead hours,
the slow sun singes the backs of skinny curs
slinking next to stucco walls.
Everyone else sleeps. It is siesta,
time to digest fried cod or black beans,
or slip into a cool, dark church,
or make love under a slow, rotating ceiling fan.

Robert left this morning
without waking me
or saying goodbye.
We never make love.
We are polite.

This time of day justifies loneliness.
No one is walking in pairs,
talking to neighbors.
Jason sleeps in my arms as heat
fills the sac of afternoon
and drips into the street like thick jelly.

Flies swarm around invisible phantoms
who have lately become my friends.

The squatters across the street hide
in thin slices of shadow.
By the wall of the vacant house,
Pregnant One curls half way around her belly
like a rubbery pod, split, guarding a single seed.
Black Man has crawled under the porch.
I don't see Red Coat. I hope she's moved on
down the coast. I don't like her.
She's snooty, stuck up, never shares.
She'll be back, strutting red queen
in her red coat, wearing her red anger
inside out. One day she will burn up.

And there is a new one I have not named.
She lies next to the hot wall,
a heap of dirty rags fermenting.

Screamer is probably under the canal bridge
spreading her diseases, hissing
at plump rats that crawl under her skirt.
The Gimp leans against a shed drinking *pinga*.

When night rises from the sea and swallows the sun,
cools and explodes perfumed blossoms into the air,
the street will come alive again.
I will shift Jason to the other breast and wonder
why I am on this balcony. I will wonder why
you leave early, Robert, and come home late.

Lying next to me this morning,
your sandy curls were bent
the wrong way on the pillow.
I wanted to touch them,
smooth them into the right direction.
Your wonderful eyes were shut
and I was glad.
When they are open,

I search to see me reflected.
I'm not there.
Nothing is there.

You are polite.
I am polite.
How terrible it is to be polite
among friends,
even worse among lovers.

Driving across country
cutting a path through
Nebraska cornfields,
we pulled off the highway
and made love.
We weren't polite.
We bought ice cream cones,
made love again.
Your kisses were pistachio nut,
sweet, wet.

○

I pace on my stone balcony,
five steps to the right . . .
five steps to the left . . .
Sometimes I stop and sway,
shifting my weight, rocking
back and forth, rocking
Jason into deeper sleep.

Sometimes I pace until
the corner bakery lights
turn on—Paderia Superior
five steps to the right . . .
five steps to the left . . .
It is a cramped world.

Sometimes I think of Velox,
the white bear in the Denver Zoo,

the oldest bear in captivity,
who paced his stone universe
over twenty years
five steps to the right . . .
five steps to the left . . .

He'd stop and sway, swing
his heavy pendulum head
back and forth,
back and forth,
then throw his nose high
in the air hoping
to catch a cold current,
breathe in a memory of ice,
frozen stepping stones
across impossible places,
a way out.

He paced three generations
of Sunday picnics, pulverizing
peanuts under his paws,
smelling only cotton candy,
popcorn, old ladies' lavender,
the zoo keeper's oily hair,
his own steaming body,
unwashed fur.
He paced through the Depression,
World War II, the Happy Days,
five steps to the right . . .
five steps to the left . . .

I never wanted to look at the blind bear,
his eyes frozen white, and so I'd hide
behind the fortress of my father's leg.
I hated Sunday picnics at the park.

I am not blind like Velox.
I have eyes and from my balcony I see
the whole world with all its comings and goings,
its little dramas and little heroes scurrying

to and fro dragging about old fears and taboos,
wearing tattered ancestral costumes
of unfinished desires, things left unsaid, undone.
How courageous are these heroes!

What of those who simply survive,
like Black Man, Gimp and Pregnant One,
who somehow get caught along the way,
whose slow footsteps lead nowhere?
Their eyes peer out of blameless bodies
that wear hand-me-downs of circumstance,
a ragbag of something gone wrong.
How courageous it is to peer at the world
through the cracks.

It takes courage to see and not understand.
It takes courage to see and to understand.
It takes courage not to see at all.
It takes courage to be a blind, white bear.
It takes courage to take one step in the dark.

o

I watch the Gimp mount Pregnant One.
Bracing himself on her swollen belly,
his shrunken left leg dangling
around her naked hip,
he tunnels through her layers.
It is over in seconds.
Neither one will remember.

Pregnant One forgot where she laid
her last baby. In the sand by the sea?
By some rocks? A crack in a wall someplace
down the coast? A doorway? Someplace dark—
someplace dark that smelled so bad, she said.

Pregnant One looks sick, waxy yellow.
I think she has toxemia.
She paces in the vacant courtyard

behind the wall
on fluid-filled legs
callused as a pachyderm's.
The baby lies low and heavy
in her spreading pelvis.
Soon another mucous pod
will drop onto the sour earth,
vibrate with life,
throb with expectation,
blinking, wet,
its small fish mouth
searching,
opening and closing
around its new air,
around nothing there,
waiting, waiting,
waiting for a shaft of light
to give it warmth.

o

It is beginning to cool.
Ocean breezes blow in the scent
of salt and fish, the smell
of beginnings and births,
memories trapped in our cells.
When I shut my eyes
like Velox, I remember something old.
I feel my inner tides pull me
back into a deep place
where I am neither fish nor plant,
but water, separated from water
by the thinnest membrane,
a transparent window
through which I look,
sometimes in, sometimes out,
it makes no difference,
and I move with the breathing
of unseen lungs.

Rosa is cooking black beans.
She is always cooking black beans,
boiling them black,
breaking their corneas,
splitting their soft souls.
She throws in crushed garlic,
dismembers a chicken,
saves the head and
sucks out the eyes and brains
with a pointed tongue,
peels the wrinkled claws,
gnaws the knuckles,
sprinkles salt in the doorway
to keep out The Devil.

I do not feel like eating.
I will put Jason to sleep and wait
for the moon to climb to my balcony,
to find and transform me.

o

Once I caught the moon
     and swallowed it,
held it captive
     in my belly,
let it rise
     to great roundness,
stretching skin
     to pearly whiteness,
thin, so thin,
     the moonlight
          shone through
and lighted up the world.

II. *Moonrise*

Now night.
I'm moonpainted.
Pearly iridescence
drenches my shoulders
liquid silver,
turns me into a goddess.

○

The blind white bear, a pale glow
in his patch of moonlight
commands a dark world.

Out of the night shadows,
Black Man glows blue, moves
gracefully as an iridescent dolphin
in a black sea.
He is a silent blue god, shimmering
silver and mica, his hands of light
drifting like sea fans—
slow speech in a liquid world.

Why do we fear you, Black Man?
Without the moon, you are invisible.
We hide in shadows with our black deeds,
believe we are unseen, yet
you are there transparent in the dark
knowing our secrets.

Why do we fear black?
Do we remember the light dimming,
obscuring form and face,
the finality of coins placed
on thin eyelids,
the closing of a coffin lid,
a black eternity?

Oh dear, oh dear.

"The light of the body
is in the eye."
Isn't it?

Below the balcony I see
a snail suctioned to earth,
caught in moonlight
midway across the patio,
like a thief carrying away
a giant gray pearl
on his back.

He fears his moment under the moon,
fears the moonbeam
will boil him, burn through
his porcelain shell.
Like a blind man feeling his way,
he swings his rubber trunk
side to side, searching
protection in the ivy.
He drags his soft underbelly
across the flagstone desert, endless,
sloughing skin, wetness, flecks
of phosphorous cells,
leaves behind a silver trail,
satin rivers, mercurial threads
crisscrossing other paths.
By morning, the mesh of iridescence
is a tight tapestry.
The snail coils in camouflage
under a geranium leaf
and does not see his handiwork.

o

Under the moon in our night kingdoms,
Black Man and I, the snail and Velox,
may weep silver tears,
but our weave is tight
and we shine like gods.

And where are you, Robert? In whose kingdom?

Next door is a spinster, Solterona,
an aging *senhorita*
bony and bent as an insect.
Her balcony is parallel to mine, but
she never steps onto it. She paces
behind the closed balcony doors
long into the night.

Once there were no balconies.
A Latin lady, pasty-skinned,
imprisoned in interior courtyards,
her mind locked in illiteracy
and urges bound by satin laces,
stitched fly-away birds in needlepoint
and repeated her prayers.
Perspiration ran rivers down
aching thighs underneath
petticoats and hot dresses.
She sat so motionless among
garden statues, a passing bird
might fancy her—a perch.

Below her window, Don Juan warbled,
strummed guitar, sang of love,
thought it a pity he couldn't see
with his own dear eye, the lady swoon,
hear her breathless sigh.
So he built her a balcony,
a fool's mistake,
for then she eyed the stable boy,
lowered her fan,
brushed the birds off her shoulders,
waited for Carnival, put on the mask,
slipped into the steaming stable
unnoticed.

o

But Solterona
closes the balcony doors
not to see the moon,

folds in on herself
like a grasshopper,
eyes solid black,
no moving rings of light,
antennae stiff
as dead grass.
Loveless, unlovable,
she bleeds bile
through her wings
staining herself
tobacco brown.
It's her only food.
Under the sheets, she
rubs her legs together
looking for music.

Good night, Robert . . . wherever you are.

III. *The New Day*

There is a gasp before dawn,
before the light splits
along the edge of old night,
a silent moment
when birds fold the chill
under their wings and wait,
a filling of the lung
before the song,
an intake of air
before the ah-h-h.
Then comes the light, again
the miracle.
Even the wet grass still pressed
in the shape of doe and fawn
stands up a blade at a time
to greet the sun.

I open my balcony doors.
The first breath of cool morning
is the wake-up splash for the soul.
From Paderia Superior, the corner bakery,
I smell hot French rolls buttering the air,
roasting coffee beans, the fishy sea,
dew-drenched mango and hanging guavas,
dark soil overturned by night worms.
Sometimes, I smell soapy clothes or
breezy sheets, sometimes,
strong oily hair tonic and sweet cologne
on the old man who strolls
to the bakery for his morning paper.
Sometimes, incense, smoking candles
and whispered novenas breathe out
from the open door of the church
and catch the high currents
that ring the city.

Grandmother taught me a prayer once.
     "Father we thank thee for the night . . .
      And for the pleasant morning light . . ."
I can't remember the rest.
I wish I could.

It is open market day, the *feira*.
Jason and I will shop . . . for trivia,
perhaps cut flowers, a ripe papaya,
a pair of booties, a new comb.
Rosa will buy the rice and beans
and see to the slaughter and
pluck of our daily fare.

I will move in the river
of shopping bags, fleshy bottoms
and strong, brown arms reaching
across oceans of oranges,
red apple patches and green-leafy stalls.
I'll move through scattered eyes, and the
flies over kilos of spices, slippery squid,
hairy brown roots, straw-matted eggs
and dung-matted dogs looking for scraps.

o

By noon, the *feira* will be gone,

packed up in trucks, the street swept clean,
and Rosa, Lupa, Maria, Dalva—all
the neighborhood *criadas,* will cook
feijoada, soupy black beans,
black beans, black beans.

Once on market day, I saw an avalanche of
oranges . . .

Small, barely dry,
his fish mouth wet and gulping,
a toddler, unattended
by his nanny,

13

reached for the oily
orange globes, enticing
as glass bubbles that bobbed
in his old watery world
and popped without reason.

One orange rolled down
the cobbled mountain,
fell to the ground,
out of place now, separate,
a disorder, something wrong.
The toddler, on tip-toe, tried
to put it back where it belonged,
tried to right the wrong.
One by one the oranges fell, swarmed
around his feet like things alive.
Then rolled the avalanche of oranges.

He stood ankle deep
in confusion.
Slowly, slowly, like a convalescent,
he picked up one
orange at a time,
put it back on the table.
And so it began.
He grasped spheres too big for his hands,
juggled planets in clumsy palms,
trying so hard to do the right thing
a fistful at a time.

○

At breakfast this morning, Robert,
the table stretched between us
like a red-checkered island,
you on one side
I on the other,
two ship-wrecked people marooned,
looking out in opposite directions,
searching a horizon,
hoping for a rescue.

This is garbage day.
Rosa bundles special treats
and puts them in the garbage can
for the squatters.
It is more than their usual daily fare.
Still they will dig to the bottom
for rotten food—chicken bones,
orange peels tossed in coffee grounds,
ashes, fish entrails, grease,
spoiled vegetables.

I remember something rotten . . .

When I was a child,
the vegetable bin in the Holly Street house
was a thing of terror, there by the screen door,
full of decapitated potato heads with puckery noses,
wrinkled and warty, like Mr. Pope in father's office.
Tendrils sprouted from caved-in foreheads, reached out
of the bin to grab me—to lift my skirt when I walked by.
Potato eyes wept, squinted, peered at me
from all sides, like Mr. Pope, who reached out
and pulled me to him in his swivel chair,
pinched my nose too hard, made my eyes water,
lifted my skirt with a white, hooked finger.

Under potatoes lay gray, furry balls of mysterious
mounds—apples, maybe, onions or lemons—consumed
by mold that coughed spores in the air if the bin
jiggled, and black-spotted pumpkins sunk in the middle,
oozed, stuck there with dark juices. Old puffs grew whiskers
and thin wispy hairs, coated plums flat like tongues,
crouched behind the heads, smelling so bad.
Mr. Pope opened his mouth to show me his gold tooth,
said I could have it if I let him kiss me, and when I
said no, he gave me a penny, laughed till he coughed
and turned red as a beet.

o

Rosa says, "We never die from bad food.
We die from no food."

No food to grow the bones,
feed the spirit,
nourish a marriage.

What is buried
has already been eaten.
The rinds are left,
the fruit bruised, spoiled.
The fallen pips
host maggots.

From the balcony, I see the squatters
crowding around the garbage can.
Red Coat is back, grabbing what she can
and stuffing her red pockets.
She shakes her fist and shouts
obscenities at me. "Sugar!
Where's the *açucar, bruxa?* Sweet!
I want something sweet, *doce!*"

I wonder if sweet could put out her fire.
I wonder if I should wear a red coat,
turn my anger inside out, let my flames
leap from my button holes, hidden pockets,
tight seams. I am burning up.
I wonder how the blind, white bear
survived the summer heat.

O

"Grandmother, why do I have to look
at the blind, white bear?"

"To learn something. Velox is our teacher.
He is our mirror, our reflection.
What we see in the bear
is what we see in ourselves."

"What do you see, Grandmother?"

"When I was young, I saw his captivity,
his frustration. Maybe because of Velox,

I did not want to see any man or animal suffer,
lose his freedom, his chance to grow
and be fulfilled.

"Lately, I see his great beauty.
I feel his strength and courage.
I understand that he is more
than a blind, white bear.
He is God's idea . . . just like me . . .
wonderfully made.

"I feel part of him is not here
at all . . . but dreaming somewhere
far away where it is beautiful,
where he is free, where he has always
been free . . . where he can run again,
without pain in his old knees,
and where he can see and understand
his own perfect reflection
in the universe.
To me, Velox is a messenger,
a white angel."

○

What should I name the newest beggar
in the family of squatters?
I never saw her arrive.
One day she was simply there
crumpled against the wall,
wadded up like a brown paper sack.
She is like something left over,
discarded, thrown away.
I never see her eat.
The only thing that moves
are her eyes. They follow
the people on the street,
but no one seems to see her.
Sometimes I wonder if she is real.
Maybe I should call her The Watcher.
I wonder if she watches me.

IV. *Afternoon*

People are running down the street,
all except Senhor Petrovsky,
old Russian photographer, who shuffles
in purple felt slippers to the *paderia*
for his vanilla ice cream cone.
It must be exactly noon.
Careful, Senhor Petrovsky,
step on a crack,
you'll break your mother's back.
Too late. Too late.

An ocean breeze ruffles his thin white hair
and I remember the blind, white bear,
his hair blowing the wrong way by a hot wind,
padding softly in his white bear slippers
going nowhere, no where.

Something has happened by the canal.

Old Legs is awake.
He hears the commotion
and struggles to his feet.
Old Legs is all one color.
Once his rags were red or blue.
Now they blend.
Where does his sleeve end
and his arm begin?
Where does his arm end
and his thin walking stick begin?
Where does his walking stick end?

o

It is getting hotter.
I sit on my balcony
and watch lizards melting
on the sidewalk.

The mid-day dragon awakens,
straddles the street,
blows her fiery breath
through stucco canyons.

The street is empty.
Everyone is at the canal
except Pregnant One
who lies by the wall
panting,
waving flies away
from her lips
with a newspaper.

Water runs underneath my shirt.
Too hot to nurse Jason.
The rivers in my breast
have dried up,
leave curdled canyons
empty, shrinking.
My breasts hang
like dried cod.

Who is walking down the street
dragging burlap bags
across the melted lizards?
A charcoal band of twisted sticks
already burnt up.
Three tots trail a father
who carries a newborn
dry as a weed.
His arms do not cradle
for milk.

They found you dead, Maria,

under the bridge,
your legs draining down the clay banks
into the canal, a cotton shift stretched
over a swollen belly, hiked up to your hips,

breasts, once soft, comforting,
a pillow for so many friends, now
lifeless bladders falling outward,
flies buzzing around dried spit
at the corners of your open mouth.
Someone probably stole your gold
front tooth.

Your friends have left our neighborhood,
except Rosa. She calls you a *puta* even now,
says an Evil One got into your body, ate
your soul when you were in a trance
working magic for Lupa.
I told Rosa you were sick, needed help.
She said you were crazy, had fits
from drinking *pinga.*
"Maria is possessed," she said.

When you went to jail, your friends
went through your things—took it all.
Rosa took your transistor radio, a pair of thongs,
your Jesus Christ calendar. Lupa took your wooden
cigar box, a plate and a cup, some plastic roses.
Ernestina got the leftovers.
No one touched the Macumba things,
afraid they might hold an old hex,
one meant for a patron, priest, jailer, judge,
a *senhora,* someone's lover.

When you were lifted from the canal, your hair
dripping with putrid water, was anyone watching
from the shadows? Was anyone standing
on the bridge when you were carried up the banks?
Did anyone think to fill in the indentation
of your shape—your cast left in the clay?
I hope you were found with your eyes shut, Maria,
not open, staring face to face at your final moment,
your final curse—the centuries
stamped in your eye.

o

Where are you, Robert?
I want to tell you about Maria.
I want to ask
if you pace on a balcony
somewhere,
if everyone has a balcony
where he views the world
and interprets life
and death.

Do you remember the mummies in Guanajuato?

I did not know those mummies
laid out
in glass cages
untitled.
Some say they died in 1905
of influenza.
Who could tell?
The fever is gone now,
that's for sure.

They all looked alike,
those papier mâché dolls,
tobacco-stained, unfinished,
unpainted, badly needing patching
and plumping, spackle
and new toes.

Some wore leather shoes,
knee socks fallen to the ankles,
boxer shorts, boots
without laces.
Most were naked—the women
with crossed arms
suspended
over sunken wombs,
the men still guarding
their jewels in case
there is a life after death.

The babies were bonneted
except the tiniest one,
"The Smallest Mummy in the World,"
a grasshopper, forever crouching
on legs never unfolded.

But it was the urgency
in the open mouths that left
us wondering if each one had
a last word, a thought, a warning,
a reckoning, a confession.
The tongue stood stiff,
charred in its hole, suspended,
a black weed in a windless cave,
a silent oracle.

○

Robert, we never argue.
It's your closed mouth,
your stiff tongue
I fear the most.

○

Grandmother said no one remembered hearing
the white bear utter a sound
for twenty years.

Before he died, he roared once, a scream heard
over the city.

○

Screamer is back from under the canal.
Too many police.
She's raving, tears at her face,
pulls her hair, beats her temples
with closed fists.
She screams for me.
She is my howl.

V. *Evening Again*

The sun has slipped
behind the sea.
The round, white moon
waits.

Between night and day, the lull
is like holding the breath,
the pause between inhale and exhale,
a question, a silent sob.

Soon night will rise from the sea
like a great wing
and curl the day close
into a soft dark body.

○

The squatters have awakened from siesta.
Gimp is wearing a lady's floppy
beach hat—blown in from somewhere.
A headless hat is a senseless thing,
and so the Gimp crowns himself
a king, or queen, the clown, the fool.
He waves his crutch—a broken broom—
high in the air, directs the traffic,
hops and falls. Without his crutch
he crawls and lets the beggars poke him,
boot him in the rear, and when
he yelps like a dog, they laugh and shout.

Even the seam in the Watcher's face
splits into a toothy smile.

From my balcony I see the piebald world,
knots and clumps, lines and dots
of dappled flesh, a busy raggle-taggle,
so singular, so alike, so connected,

an after-school centipede of navy blue
school children wearing knee socks,

shapeless girls shivering from the beach,
bodies sleek and wet as sea otters,
their older sisters oily brown
with rounded hips, perfumed hair
and everywhere blossoms open,
exotic, ready . . .

across the street, the lady
in the white nightgown who flutters
in her window like a white moth,
her palms pressed white
against the pane.

"Grandmother, I think the white bear is lonely."

"The Indians say that loneliness
is the one thing
all men share and understand.
It is the driving force not to be lonely,
but to be loved, touched somehow."

"It would be terrible not to be loved."

"Remember, whatever we see in the white bear
is reflected in us as well.
He is our double, a mirror of us.
The Indians call it sympathetic magic."

"I love that old, blind, white bear, Grandmother."

"Love is reflected in love.
Indeed that is magic."

○

The old bear finally died,
shut his inner eyes for good.
Hundreds came to say goodbye—

old, young, very young,
doctors, lawyers, social workers,
priests, teachers, gardeners, housewives,
grandmothers—they all came,
three generations. They all came.
They all wept.

It was the passing of an old friend,
the passing of a portion of ourselves.
We stood around the empty stone shelf
where Velox had paced for over twenty years.

I remember now.
I stood in the crowd,
one with them, ringed
by sympathetic magic,
all of us
individual universes
shining like tiny mirrors,
reflecting each other,
continually turning, catching
the glint of another soul,
each of us sending out
our own beam of light,
if only for a moment,
dissolving loneliness
with love.

○

Tonight the moon is an open eye,
wide and bright and full of wonder.
It is the largest eye into which I beam,
eye to eye, blood tide high.

Sometimes,
I beam into the hummingbird's eye,
travel that thin light to a single source,
a common pool of divine stuff,
a convergence of all roads
through all the eyes of every creature

down to the tiniest mite.
Were I to look into his microscopic eye,
there too, I could enter in, reach that source
and understand we are all simply Life expressed,
part of a Grand Design,
animated and individualized
by some kind of Mind, the Creator's
special Magic.

○

Sometimes, the whys that clack together
like dry sticks, meaningless,
disappear, and for a moment,
strangers and full moons, black beans
and beggars, love songs of crickets,
a three-legged dog and dew-drenched webs,
all at once . . . All . . . at once, make sense.
The fat and gristle that is me,
the barrier against this *something*
that is really no thing at all,
becomes transparent as a doughnut hole
without the doughnut.
Between heartbeats,
I fall into this hole with the All,
and the crickets, to find we shout
to each other without mouths,
breathe without lungs, embrace without arms,
see everything without names,
love without walls.

I do not understand why I am who I am,
why I sit on this balcony tonight
nursing Jason, feeling full of the moon,
full of light, seeing part of myself
in everyone else, sharing this moment

in time, why I am not the one
sleeping next to the wall across the street.

Tonight a speck of me is in everyone else.

I am Red Coat
    Screamer
    Black Man
    Watcher
    Senhor Petrovsky
    The Gimp
    Old Legs
    Grasshopper

I am Maria
    Burnt Sticks
    Blue God
    Goddess
    White Moth
    Pregnant One
    Mother
    Snail

I am Velox, the blind, white bear
    Part of the Original Light,
    the living liquid light
    that long ago spilled itself
    and spattered tiny universes
    of individuals into the darkness
    to give it beauty and meaning.

○

Jason, my tiny universe,
my tiny bead of light,
the night is cool out on the balcony,

perfumed from blossoms too fragile
for the day, creamy white,
like my nectar rich and sweet.
Together we are cradled by unseen arms.

Father we thank thee for the night,
and for the pleasant morning light . . .
and for the Light,
for the Light, for the bear,
the white bear, The Light,
The White
Light.

Announcing the 1994

Pearl
Chapbook Contest

Judge: ANN MENEBROKER

○○○○○○○○○○○○○○○○○○○○○○○○○○○

$100 PRIZE

*Winner will also receive publication,
50 copies, and a foreword
by Ann Menebroker*

○○○○○○○○○○○○○○○○○○○○○○○○○○○

SUBMISSION GUIDELINES

MANUSCRIPTS should include a title page with the author's name, address and phone number; an acknowledgment page listing previously published poems; 20-24 pages of poetry; and an SASE for a reply or the return of manuscript. Manuscripts should be typed, pages numbered, and **name should appear on title page only.** Clear photo-copies and computer print-outs are acceptable. We will consider simul-taneous submissions, but ask that you notify us if your manuscript is accepted elsewhere.

$10 ENTRY FEE includes a copy of the winning chapbook. All other proceeds go to the continuing publication of *Pearl*.

JUDGING: The selection of manuscripts for final judging will be made by the editors of *Pearl*. All entries will be read anonymously.

SUBMISSION PERIOD: Manuscripts will be accepted from May 1 through July 1, 1994. The winner will be announced and manuscripts returned in November.

SEND SUBMISSIONS TO: Pearl Chapbook Contest, 3030 E. Second St., Long Beach, CA 90803.

CAROLYN EVANS CAMPBELL is a native Coloradan and graduate of the University of Colorado. For several years she lived in in South America and later in California where she taught school and worked on a writing career. Her first book of poetry, *Waiting for the Condor,* is a collection of published poems, many of which reflect her South American experience. Her work has appeared in numerous anthologies and small presses, including *Nebo, Midland Review, Slow Dancer, Bogg, Sycamore Review, Karamu, Poetry San Francisco, Poetry USA, Madison Review,* and *Visions International.* She has also won many awards including first place for the National Writer's Poetry Prize in 1991. She presently teaches in adult education in the Denver Public Schools, with Elderhostel, and in various gifted and talented programs in poetry and creative writing.